ZRJC

TREME FISH

Sturgeon

BY S.L. HAMILTON

Visit us at
www.abdopublishing.com

Published by Abdo Publishing Company, a division of ABDO, PO Box 398166, Minneap
Minnesota 55439. Copyright ©2015 by Abdo Consulting Group, Inc. International
copyrights reserved in all countries. No part of this book may be reproduced in any fo
without written permission from the publisher. A&D Xtreme™ is a trademark and logo
Abdo Publishing Company.

Printed in the United States of America, North Mankato, Minnesota.
052014
092014

Editor: John Hamilton
Graphic Design: Sue Hamilton
Cover Design: Sue Hamilton
Cover Photo: Alamy
Interior Photos: Alamy-pgs 28-29; AP-pgs 26, 27 & 32; Corbis-pgs 18-19; Getty-pgs 4-
8-9, 10 (bottom illustration), 13, 15, 16-17 & 24-25; Glow Images-pgs 10-11, 12 &
30-31; iStock-pgs 6-7; National Geographic-pgs 20-21; Thinkstock-pgs 1, 2-3, 10
(sturgeon illustration) & 14; U.S. Fish and Wildlife Service-pgs 22-23; Wisconsin Histo
Society-pg 21 (inset).

Websites
To learn more about Xtreme Fish, visit booklinks.abdopublishing.com. These links are
routinely monitored and updated to provide the most current information available.

Library of Congress Control Number: 2014932244

Cataloging-in-Publication Data

Hamilton, S. L.
Sturgeon / S. L. Hamilton.
p. cm. -- (Xtreme fish)
Includes index.
ISBN 978-1-62403-451-0
1. Sturgeons--Juvenile literature.   2. Marine animals--Juvenile literature.   I. Title.
597--dc23

2014932244

Contents

Sturgeon

Sturgeon are an ancient type of fish that swam in the days of the dinosaurs. They are protected by armor-like bony plates. They may grow to monstrous sizes, some reaching 20 feet (6 m) in length.

XTREME FACT – Scientists estimated that a lake sturgeon caught in 1953 was 150 years old. If so, it would have been alive when the Lewis & Clark Expedition explored the newly purchased land in the central and northwestern United States.

Sturgeon may live incredibly long lives, sometimes more than 100 years. This is good because it takes up to 20 years for a sturgeon to reach adulthood. However, over-fishing has reduced the sturgeon population greatly. Many species are in danger of being gone forever.

Species & Location

There are about 26 species of sturgeon. They have existed nearly unchanged for about 135 million years. Their unique bodies are covered in bony plates called scutes (pronounced "sk-yo͞ots").

XTREME FACT–
Sturgeon are known as "living fossils."

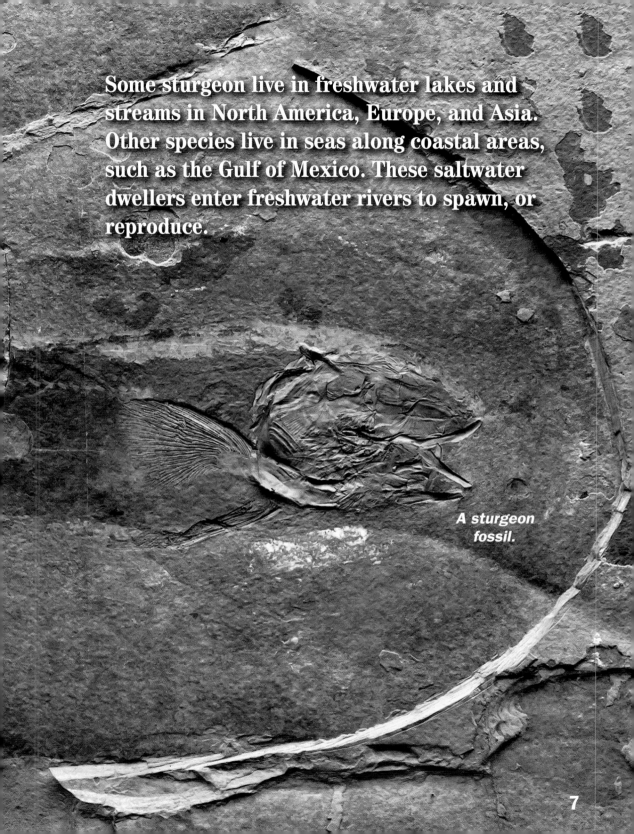

Some sturgeon live in freshwater lakes and streams in North America, Europe, and Asia. Other species live in seas along coastal areas, such as the Gulf of Mexico. These saltwater dwellers enter freshwater rivers to spawn, or reproduce.

A sturgeon fossil.

Size

Sturgeon differ in size, depending on the species. One of the largest lake-dwelling fish is the white sturgeon.

In 2012, anglers in British Columbia, Canada, caught and released a white sturgeon estimated to weigh 1,100 pounds (499 kg). One of the largest beluga sturgeon ever caught weighed 3,463 pounds (1571 kg). These fish are big and powerful.

XTREME FACT – A sturgeon grows faster when the water temperature is cooler, in the low 50s to mid-60s degrees Fahrenheit (10-18°C) range.

Sturgeon have remained nearly unchanged in appearance for millions of years. They still look like their ancient ancestors, with rows of bony plates called scutes.

Sturgeon are one of the few sea creatures that have survived since the age of dinosaurs. Sturgeon have existed for about 135 million years.

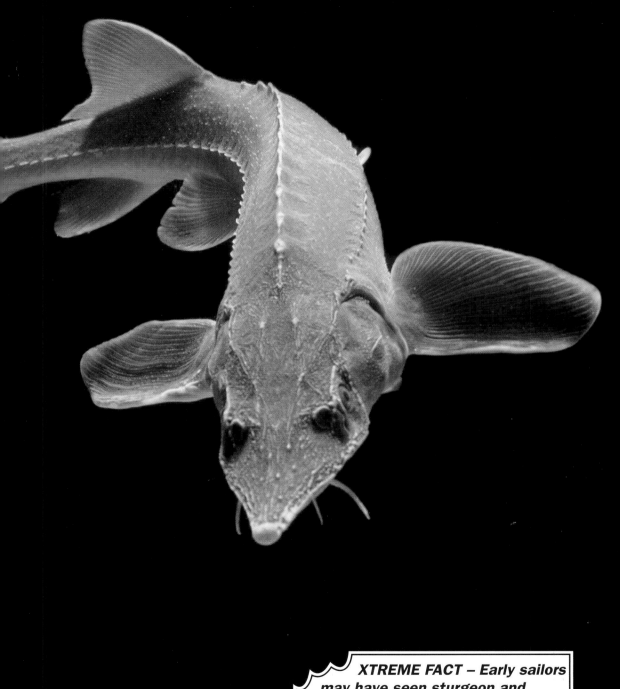

XTREME FACT – Early sailors may have seen sturgeon and thought the big fish were mermaids.

Barbels & Mouth

Sturgeon do not have teeth. They have blunt snouts, or rostrum, with whisker-like barbels. Their four barbels are equipped with taste buds to help them find food in murky water.

A sturgeon's snout is used to stir up mud as it searches for food. Sturgeon travel along the river or sea floor using their barbels to search for small fish, shrimp, crayfish, snails, clams, insect larvae, and worms. They grasp food with their lips and then vacuum it up into their mouths. Their food is swallowed whole.

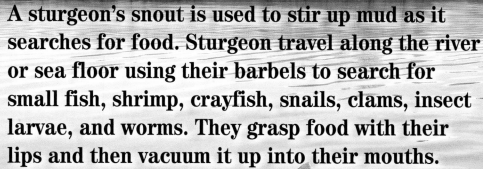

A sturgeon does not have scales. It is covered with bony, scale-like plates called scutes. This protective "armor" covers its sides and back in five rows. Usually, the bottom of a sturgeon does not have scutes.

Scutes

XTREME FACT – Very old sturgeon have worn down their scutes so much that their skin looks smooth.

When a sturgeon is young, these plates are sharp and pointed for protection. As the fish ages, the plates wear down and become more rounded and smooth.

A young sturgeon's scutes are sharp and pointed for protection.

Beluga Sturgeon

Beluga sturgeon are huge. Some sources state that beluga may weigh as much as 5,953 pounds (2,700 kg) and can reach a length of 28 feet (8.5 m). These fish are found in the Caspian, Black, and Adriatic Seas near Russia. Beluga have been hunted for their "roe," or eggs. It is called caviar, and is sold for up to $300 an ounce.

Beluga sturgeon may live up to 150 years. However they are slow to grow and mature. Because of this and overfishing, they are now a protected species. Neither beluga caviar nor meat are allowed to be imported into the United States. It is against the law to intentionally kill these endangered fish in the wild.

XTREME FACT – Beluga sturgeon are not related to beluga whales. The word "beluga" comes from the Russian word for white.

White Sturgeon

White sturgeon are actually gray or brown in color. They are found in coastal waters from Alaska to Baja, California, and in freshwater as far inland as Montana.

White sturgeon may grow to 20 feet (6 m) in length and weigh up to 1,800 pounds (816 kg). This makes them one of the biggest fish in North America. They are an anadromous fish, meaning they spend much of their lives in saltwater, but swim up freshwater rivers to spawn.

XTREME FACT – *White sturgeon have poor eyesight. They use their sense of smell to find and suck up their prey from the water bottom.*

Lake Sturgeon

Lake sturgeon are a freshwater species living in the Great Lakes and other lakes and streams of eastern North America. These fish are not supersized like their beluga and white sturgeon cousins, but may still weigh up to 200 pounds (91 kg).

Lake sturgeon use their long snouts to dig in muddy bottoms for worms, leeches, and insect larvae. Their rubbery lips surround and suck up their live prey. They are very large fish living on very tiny prey.

XTREME FACT – In the late 1800s, millions of pounds of lake sturgeon were taken from America's Great Lakes. By the early 1900s, the slow-growing fish had nearly died out. The sturgeon population never returned to what it once was. Today, fishing for lake sturgeon is very limited.

Shortnose Sturgeon

Shortnose sturgeon are named for their less-than-lengthy noses. What they do not have in nose length, they make up for in mouth width. Shortnose sturgeon have big mouths that take up a major portion of their lower faces.

Shortnose sturgeon weigh only about 8 pounds (3.6 kg), with a record size of 11 pounds (5 kg). Shortnoses live along the east coast of North America. Shortnose sturgeon are endangered.

XTREME FACT–
Shortnose sturgeon are "anadromous." They live their lives in saltwater and swim to freshwater to spawn.

Shovelnose Sturgeon

Shovelnose sturgeon have unique shovel-shaped snouts. Also, unlike other sturgeon, their bellies are covered in small, bony plates.

Shovelnose are the runts of the sturgeon family. Most only reach about 5 pounds (2.3 kg). A record-sized shovelnose weighed 10 pounds 12 ounces (4.88 kg). Shovelnose are strictly freshwater fish. They are found in the Mississippi and Missouri River basins in the United States. Shovelnose may be fished, although their populations are closely watched.

Attacks on Humans

Some sturgeon grow as big as great white sharks, but have no teeth and are typically not dangerous to humans. There are stories of hooked sturgeon dragging anglers underwater and drowning them. Sturgeon are also known to "breach," or jump out of the water, striking people.

It is not known why sturgeon jump, but there are several guesses:
- *A way to talk to each other*
- *Rid their bodies of parasites*
- *Spawning behavior*
- *Gulping air to equalize the pressure in their swim bladder. This helps them move to different depths in the water.*

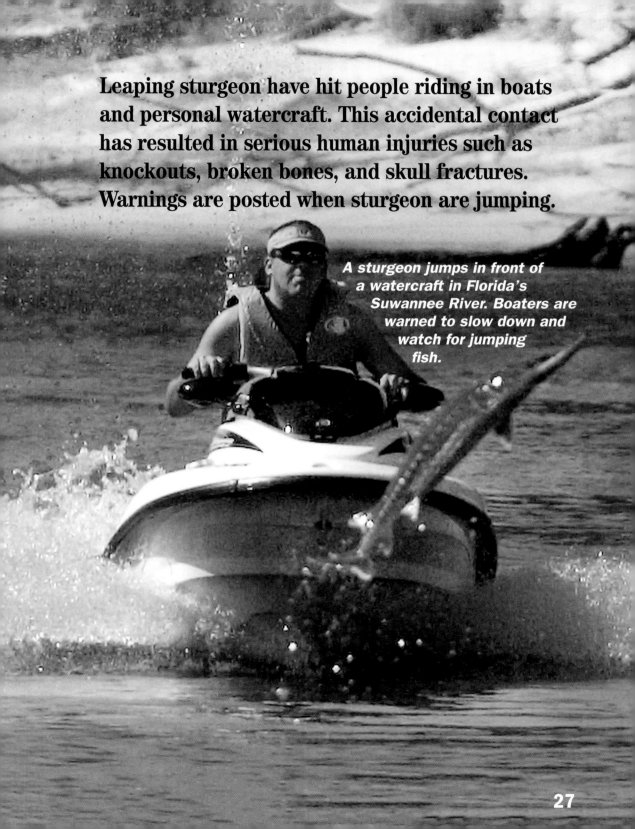

Leaping sturgeon have hit people riding in boats and personal watercraft. This accidental contact has resulted in serious human injuries such as knockouts, broken bones, and skull fractures. Warnings are posted when sturgeon are jumping.

A sturgeon jumps in front of a watercraft in Florida's Suwannee River. Boaters are warned to slow down and watch for jumping fish.

Fishing for Sturgeon

Since many sturgeon species are protected, only a very limited number of them may be fished.

For licensed anglers, sturgeon fishing is an exciting sport. When hooked, sturgeon often launch themselves into the air, or breach. Monster-sized sturgeon will jump and run, putting up an unforgettably great fight.

XTREME FACT– Because of their large size and stubborn fighting, sturgeon are sometimes called the "poor man's marlin."

Glossary

ANADROMOUS
Fish that spend much of their lives in saltwater, but swim up freshwater rivers to spawn. White sturgeon and shortnose sturgeon are anadromous.

BARBELS
Whisker-like organs found near the mouths of certain fish such as catfish and sturgeon. Barbels act as taste buds.

BREACH
When fish jump out of the water.

CAVIAR
Salted fish eggs taken from inside a female sturgeon. Caviar is considered a delicacy and is very expensive.

GREAT LAKES
The interconnected freshwater lakes of Superior, Michigan, Huron, Ontario, and Erie. They are on the border between the United States and Canada. They connect to the Atlantic Ocean via the Saint Lawrence Seaway.

LEWIS AND CLARK EXPEDITION
An exploration of the western United States, led by Meriwether Lewis and William Clark, from 1804 to 1806.

MARLIN

A sport fish that anglers hunt
because of its fierceness and
difficulty in landing, making its capture
an exciting sport.

ROE

The mass of eggs inside a fish. A female sturgeon's eggs
may make up as much as one-third of her weight.

ROSTRUM

In sturgeon, a projecting snout.

SPAWN

When fish reproduce. The female fish deposits her eggs,
usually in water, and the male fertilizes them with his sperm.

SWIM BLADDER

A sac inside the body of a fish that holds air. It is also
known as a gas bladder or air bladder. It helps a fish
adjust to different water depths.

TASTE BUDS

Organs that identify edible items. In a human, taste buds
are on the tongue.

Index